T0345245

Elegy Written in a Country Churchyard

Elegy Written in a Country Churchyard

THOMAS GRAY

WOOD ENGRAVINGS BY
AGNES MILLER PARKER

BODLEIAN
LIBRARY
PUBLISHING

Contents

Loss Transformed
CAROL RUMENS

From the time of the steam-powered printing
press to today's shiny electronic screens, Thomas
Gray's *Elegy Written in a Country Churchyard* has been
loved, quoted and memorized by readers, admired
by poets, evaluated by critics and reissued by
publishers. Less often remarked upon is its vividly
pictorial narrative, which has consistently attracted
artist–illustrators, among them Richard Bentley
(the earliest), William Blake, Charles Landseer
and John Constable. The wood engravings by
Agnes Miller Parker, originally made for the 1938
publication of the *Elegy* by the Limited Editions
Club and reproduced in this book, are an exciting
twentieth-century addition to the corpus.

Wood engraving and verse-making are not entirely dissimilar arts. They both rely on excision – the un-inked lines, the silent spaces. Material has to be discarded, a physical process for the engraver, but no less essential for the poet, who, with invisible cutting tools, condenses language into rhythmical patterns that lift it from the page. Gray's deployment of stanza form, metre and rhyme, and Parker's bold outlines and contrasts, demonstrate that, in the discipline of omission, as well as in their showing and telling, both artist and poet are masters.

Agnes Miller Parker (1895–1980) was born in Irvine, Ayrshire, and trained at the Glasgow School of Art; her early paintings were influenced by the Vorticist movement. She developed her technique of wood engraving by learning from the English printmaker and sculptor Gertrude Hermes (1901–1983). Based in England for most of her life, during the early 1930s she worked for the Gregynog Press in Wales with her husband, the artist William McCance. The many popular classics she illustrated include Aesop's *Fables* and Housman's *A Shropshire Lad*, novels by Thomas Hardy and works by the natural-history writer Richard Jefferies.

Parker's preliminary studies for the *Elegy*'s illustrations were made in the same churchyard, that of St Giles, Stoke Poges, in which the poem is set. Her interpretations fuse modernist and traditional styles of draftsmanship. Unexpected juxtapositions of perspective and imagery go beyond rustic narrative, sometimes to complement Gray's quatrains with further strokes of invention. Her human figures, chiefly male, are invariably seen in action: they heft hay or firewood, 'scatter plenty' to their chickens, confront authority. The social comment of the starker scenes re-emphasizes Gray's own Enlightenment values. Parker's many depictions of gravestones, literally 'en-grave-ings', poignantly record the stone-cutter's struggles with the art of inscription.

While Parker portrays the natural world with a certain vivid realism, an interesting stylization occurs when she encloses key images in leaf-like or fruit-like outlines. She helps us to read the *Elegy* as twenty-first-century conservationists, and recognize its ecological connectivity. Gray himself had a lifelong interest in botany and natural history generally; he might have appreciated Parker's shapely, vigorous representations of the fauna and flora of the Buckinghamshire country-side which, next to Cambridge, became his second home.

Born on 26 December 1716 in London's Cornhill, Thomas Gray was the fifth of twelve children, and the only one to survive infancy. His unhappily married parents were Philip Gray, a scrivener in the City of London, and Dorothy Antrobus, who co-owned a millinery business with her sister Mary. Dorothy's income supported Thomas through Eton and Cambridge, with the additional help of a scholarship to the latter. Like his old school friend Richard West (1716–1742), he initially planned to earn his living as a barrister.

'Too poor for a bribe and too proud to importune, / He had not the method of making his fortune', Gray quipped, in 'Sketch of his Own Character'. He was no entitled gentleman of leisure, although sufficiently funded to abandon law as a career and devote himself to the scholarly life at Peterhouse and, later, Pembroke College. Proficient in a range of languages, classical and modern, he composed his earliest verse in Latin. By the time he came to write the *Elegy*, possibly in the second half of 1742, he was an accomplished young poet, but not a seeker of literary fame.

The poem's popularity predated (and hastened) its publication. In 1750 Gray had sent a completed draft to another school friend, Horace Walpole (son of Sir Robert, the Whig prime minister). Horace enthusiastically circulated the poem, and a 'leak' ensued. Gray received a letter promising the *Elegy's* forthcoming appearance in a periodical, *Magazine of Magazines*. To forestall the unauthorized printing, he asked Walpole to place the poem with the publisher

Robert Dodsley, who had already anthologized some of Gray's verse.

Gray had intended his *Elegy* to remain anonymous. In the event, his anonymity was preserved only in the first edition. Dodsley's sixpenny chapbook appeared early in 1751 and had run to five printings by the year's end.

The poem continued to please an ever-widening readership. It became central to the English school curriculum, and, well into the twentieth century, generations of schoolchildren learned to recite it. Samuel Johnson, not generally an admirer of Gray's work, had noticed its universal appeal early on.

> The 'Church-yard' abounds with images which find a mirrour in every mind, and with sentiments to which every bosom returns an echo. The four stanzas beginning 'Yet even these bones' are to me original; I have never seen the notions of any other place; yet he that reads them here persuades himself that he has always felt them.'

Gray's images are almost always in motion. The arresting first stanza assembles simple descriptive statements into a flowing view. Cinematic for today's readers, it connects Gray's pastoralism to the then newly emergent English landscape movement, noted for its enthusiasm for the well-planned scene. With a daring swoop from the horizon and its small figures, ploughman and cattle, Gray reduces 'the world' to the immediate world of the poem, and then to the stanza's last echoing word, 'me', a pronoun utterly unexpected and poignant. The speaker will not reappear until stanza 24. In his modesty and wisdom, he vanishes into the darkness, leaving the poem to tread its gently majestic way unhindered by obvious self-reference.

The *Elegy* is a public poem, but it's tinged with personal emotions that do not altogether 'blush unseen'. One aspect of this sensibility shows in Gray's diction. The gracefully precise and clear descriptive language seems to lean on direct observation and reflection, and the overall poetic idiom, for all its power and ingenuity, never overwhelms the human quality of the voice. Whereas Milton's great pastoral elegy *Lycidas* declares the author's wealth of learning, Gray's *Elegy* subdues it. Mount Parnassus, the seat of poetry and music in Ancient Greece, is represented only by the Muse, lettered and 'unletter'd'. Analysis reveals rich intertextual layers, of course, but these need not be unpacked in order for the poem to communicate: it is brilliantly accessible.

The classical elegy was a sung lament with flute accompaniment. Gray's own musical effects are audible in words and phrases, and are entwined in the larger flow of syntax and stanza. The regular metre is lightened by various sound patterns into melody. So, in the opening line, a subtle alliteration suggests the uneven beat of the bell: 'The curfew *tolls* the *knell* of parting day' – a tolling that unobtrusively permeates the entire poem. In stanza 2, we can hear 'the beetle wheel[s] his droning flight' in the repeated *ee* and *whee* sounds. As the unseen flock settles to sleep, the phrase 'drowsy tinklings' softens the jingling sheep bells with beautifully realized onomatopoeia.

According to his manuscript annotations, Gray's first line takes up a trope from canto VIII of Dante's *Purgatorio*, 'the bell / which seems to mourn the dying day'. An image of resurrection is implicit in Gray's revision: the day is 'parting' rather than 'dying', with a promise of renewal that foreshadows the Epitaph's final, solidly Christian affirmation. The fading daylight streaking the west in Parker's engraving for this stanza is characteristic of her skill in capturing circadian rhythms through contrasted effects of light and dark.

Gray sometimes notices the Gothic qualities in nature, as when remarking the 'nodding beech / That wreathes its old fantastic roots so high' (stanza 26). His 'mopeing owl' (stanza 3) seems, at first, to belong to the same register. Birds, not only owls, complaining of lost love are an old poetic standby, and Gray himself had used the trope in the earlier 'Sonnet on the Death of Mr. Richard West'. But now there's a different resonance. The owl behaves like a real bird, uttering an alarm call in reaction to human presence

– a pair of mourners or lovers, as the engraving reveals. Her complaint is not a mere poeticism.

As the *Elegy* progresses, the increasingly rhetorical and metaphorical technique accommodates a more abstract argument. It emphasizes the contrast between the legacies of power and powerlessness, and allows Gray to deliver an eloquent discourse on promise unfulfilled and lives forgotten. His sentences expand and are sometimes sustained, without an end-stop, across several stanzas. The broad strokes used to evoke landscape are now applied to the human lifespan and the arc of history.

The politics are potentially radical: knowledge and talent are thwarted through social inequity. But the elegist remembers that death is the ultimate victor, and may deny fulfilment – and commemoration – to all the social classes. 'Full many a gem of purest ray serene, / The dark unfathom'd caves of ocean bear' (stanza 14) is a generality, as are the echoing third and fourth lines, 'Full many a flow'r is born to blush unseen, / And waste its sweetness on the desert air.'

The repetitive device anaphora is rhetorically persuasive, and seems to assert the pulse of a more personally felt sympathy.

In the climactic rollcall of stanza 15 Milton, interestingly, is the only poet. Although challenged by Gray's own poetics, he remained a revered influence. How cleverly 'mute' and 'inglorious' suggest their opposite qualities, eloquence and gloriousness. Originally, three Romans represented the men of achievement: Cato, Tully and Caesar. A bold revision, the appearance of Hampden and Cromwell (after Milton!) localizes the turmoil of warfare and conscience.

Gray's counter-argument that the poverty which circumscribes the 'growing virtues' of the poor equally limits their 'crimes' is his opportunity to castigate the powerful. The governing clause of stanzas 17–18, 'Their lot forbad', liberates Gray's moral imagination. Generalization is again quickened by metaphor: a simple, physical verb 'wade' as in 'wade through slaughter to a throne' evokes the depth of the shed blood, the effort of pushing ruthlessly to power through a sea of bodies. Later, in the much-quoted stanza 19, it's the first adjective in 'the madding crowd's ignoble strife' which creates the stunning effect. Gray wasn't the first poet to use 'madding': his choice is no less exemplary. It produces another of those images that are in motion, the exposed double *d* adding a wild giddiness to the more usual and somehow too decorous 'maddening'.

One of the *Elegy*'s great achievements is its easy movement between public and more personal, meditative idioms. Both are perfectly judged. Gray's voice is never too oratorical, nor too private, to leave his readers feeling excluded.

The intimate tone of the earlier quatrains returns in stanza 22 as the poem draws towards its conclusion:

> For who to dumb Forgetfulness a prey,
> This pleasing anxious being e'er resign'd,
> Left the warm precincts of the cheerful day,
> Nor cast one longing, ling'ring look behind?

Gray's question seems to address both the audience and himself. The lines tremble and loiter. He imagines the sadness of the dying as they contemplate a perhaps more frightening 'death' – that of being forgotten. Parker's interpretation is particularly striking, with its shrouded figure, a corpse or ghost, standing with its back to the viewer and looking down on the fields where work goes on as before. It reflects the significance placed in Greek epic poetry on proper funeral rites for the deceased hero–warriors. Without these, the humbler shades, too, may find no rest.

Envisioning himself among the dead, Gray surprises us with a conversation in which 'some hoary-headed Swain' answers enquiries about the deceased. This bold move, perhaps a little self-mocking, leads seamlessly into a further new mood and 'voice', that of the Epitaph. Is the latter simply Gray's epitaph on himself? Could the wistfully lingering young man he portrays embody another identity – that of Gray's beloved friend

Richard West, also a poet but not well known, lost to tuberculosis at the age of 25? I think the enmeshed personification of West with Gray (bereaved and also anxious about his own future) the most apt interpretation, the key to the underlying emotional intensity of the work – and its very title. Traditionally, the elegy laments a specific individual.

Parker's visionary final image of fatherly enfolding perhaps alludes to the family scene of stanza 6, in which the gaunt-faced young farm worker, newly arrived home, has gathered up his daughter tenderly in his strong right arm. The majestic but near-organic, almost foetal, image of the godhead and the cradled adult 'child' is as confident as her animations of the natural world. It reminds us that art never merely records what is local, human and tangible. Both Gray's verse and Parker's engravings have the power to transform emptiness and loss, and make the invisible thrillingly present.

Elegy Written in a
Country Churchyard

1

The curfew tolls the knell of parting day,
The lowing herd wind slowly o'er the lea,
The plowman homeward plods his weary way,
And leaves the world to darkness and to me.

2

Now fades the glimm'ring landscape on the sight,
And all the air a solemn stillness holds,
Save where the beetle wheels his droning flight,
And drowsy tinklings lull the distant folds;

3

Save that from yonder ivy-mantled tow'r
The mopeing owl does to the moon complain
Of such, as wand'ring near her secret bow'r,
Molest her ancient, solitary reign.

4

Beneath those rugged elms, that yew-tree's shade,
Where heaves the turf in many a mould'ring heap,
Each in his narrow cell for ever laid,
The rude Forefathers of the hamlet sleep.

5

The breezy call of incense-breathing morn,
The swallow twitt'ring from the straw-built shed,
The cock's shrill clarion, or the echoing horn,
No more shall rouse them from their lowly bed.

6

For them no more the blazing hearth shall burn,
Or busy housewife ply her evening care:
No children run to lisp their sire's return,
Or climb his knees the envied kiss to share.

7

Oft did the harvest to their sickle yield,
Their furrow oft the stubborn glebe has broke;
How jocund did they drive their team afield!
How bow'd the woods beneath their sturdy stroke!

8

Let not Ambition mock their useful toil,
Their homely joys, and destiny obscure;
Nor Grandeur hear with a disdainful smile
The short and simple annals of the poor.

9

The boast of heraldry, the pomp of pow'r,
And all that beauty, all that wealth e'er gave,
Awaits alike th' inevitable hour.
The paths of glory lead but to the grave.

Nor you, ye Proud, impute to these the fault,
If Mem'ry o'er their tomb no trophies raise,
Where thro' the long-drawn aisle and fretted vault
The pealing anthem swells the note of praise.

11

Can storied urn or animated bust
Back to its mansion call the fleeting breath?
Can Honour's voice provoke the silent dust,
Or Flatt'ry soothe the dull cold ear of Death?

12

Perhaps in this neglected spot is laid
Some heart once pregnant with celestial fire;
Hands, that the rod of empire might have sway'd,
Or wak'd to ecstasy the living lyre.

13

But Knowledge to their eyes her ample page
Rich with the spoils of time did ne'er unroll;
Chill Penury repress'd their noble rage,
And froze the genial current of the soul.

14

Full many a gem of purest ray serene,
The dark unfathom'd caves of ocean bear:
Full many a flow'r is born to blush unseen,
And waste its sweetness on the desert air.

15

Some village-Hampden, that with dauntless breast
The little Tyrant of his fields withstood;
Some mute inglorious Milton here may rest,
Some Cromwell guiltless of his country's blood.

16

Th' applause of list'ning senates to command,
The threats of pain and ruin to despise,
To scatter plenty o'er a smiling land,
And read their hist'ry in a nation's eyes,

17

Their lot forbad: nor circumscrib'd alone
Their growing virtues, but their crimes confin'd;
Forbad to wade through slaughter to a throne,
And shut the gates of mercy on mankind,

18

The struggling pangs of conscious truth to hide,
To quench the blushes of ingenuous shame,
Or heap the shrine of Luxury and Pride
With incense kindled at the Muse's flame.

Far from the madding crowd's ignoble strife,
Their sober wishes never learn'd to stray;
Along the cool sequester'd vale of life
They kept the noiseless tenor of their way.

Yet ev'n these bones from insult to protect,
Some frail memorial still erected nigh,
With uncouth rhymes and shapeless sculpture deck'd,
Implores the passing tribute of a sigh.

Their name, their years, spelt by th' unletter'd muse,
The place of fame and elegy supply:
And many a holy text around she strews,
That teach the rustic moralist to die.

22

For who to dumb Forgetfulness a prey,
This pleasing anxious being e'er resign'd,
Left the warm precincts of the cheerful day,
Nor cast one longing, ling'ring look behind?

On some fond breast the parting soul relies,
Some pious drops the closing eye requires;
Ev'n from the tomb the voice of Nature cries,
Ev'n in our ashes live their wonted fires.

For thee, who mindful of th' unhonour'd Dead
Dost in these lines their artless tale relate;
If chance, by lonely contemplation led,
Some kindred Spirit shall inquire thy fate,

25

Haply some hoary-headed Swain may say,
'Oft have we seen him at the peep of dawn
Brushing with hasty steps the dews away
To meet the sun upon the upland lawn.

'There at the foot of yonder nodding beech
That wreathes its old fantastic roots so high,
His listless length at noontide would he stretch,
And pore upon the brook that babbles by.

'Hard by yon wood, now smiling as in scorn,
Mutt'ring his wayward fancies he would rove,
Now drooping, woeful wan, like one forlorn,
Or craz'd with care, or cross'd in hopeless love.

'One morn I miss'd him on the custom'd hill,
Along the heath and near his fav'rite tree;
Another came; nor yet beside the rill,
Nor up the lawn, nor at the wood was he;

'The next with dirges due in sad array
Slow thro' the church-way path we saw him borne.
Approach and read (for thou canst read) the lay,
Grav'd on the stone beneath yon aged thorn.'

THE EPITAPH

Here rests his head upon the lap of Earth
A youth to Fortune and to Fame unknown.
Fair Science frown'd not on his humble birth,
And Melancholy mark'd him for her own.

Large was his bounty, and his soul sincere,
Heav'n did a recompense as largely send:
He gave to Mis'ry all he had, a tear,
He gain'd from Heav'n ('twas all he wish'd) a friend.

No farther seek his merits to disclose,
Or draw his frailties from their dread abode,
(There they alike in trembling hope repose)
The bosom of his Father and his God.

This edition published in 2021 by the Bodleian Library
Broad Street, Oxford OX1 3BG
www.bodleianshop.co.uk

ISBN 978 1 85124 577 2

Introduction © Carol Rumens, 2021
Illustrations © The Estate of Agnes Miller Parker, 2021

Illustrations are from *Elegy Written in a Country Church-yard* by Thomas Gray;
with wood-engravings by Agnes Miller Parker.
Printed for members of the Limited Editions Club at the Raven Press,
London, 1938. Oxford, Bodleian Library, Limited Editions Club 106

All photography, unless specified, © Bodleian Library, University of Oxford, 2021

All rights reserved.

Publisher: Samuel Fanous
Managing Editor: Deborah Susman
Editor: Janet Phillips
Picture Editor: Leanda Shrimpton
Production Editor: Susie Foster
Cover design by Dot Little at the Bodleian Library
Designed and typeset by Lucy Morton of illuminati in 14 on 20 Monotype Centaur
Printed and bound in China by C&C Offset Printing Co. Ltd,
on 130 gsm Chinese Baijin pure woodfree paper

British Library Catalogue in Publishing Data
A CIP record of this publication is available from the British Library